## Otherwise Unchanged

Born in 1968, Owen Lowery was formerly a British Judo champion, but suffered a spinal injury in 1987 while competing, as a result of which he is now a ventilator-dependent C2-level tetraplegic. Since his accident Owen has gained a first-class honours degree in Humanities with the Open University, a Master's degree in Military Studies at Chester University, and a Master's degree with distinction in Creative Writing at Bolton University, where he is completing his PhD. His poetry has appeared in *PN Review*, *Stand*, and various competition anthologies. Owen's poetry often explores the relationship between natural expression and formal arrangement, and covers a wide range of personal, historical and artistic subjects. An avid football fan, Owen is a season ticket holder at Anfield and Bolton's Reebok Stadium. He enjoys blues, jazz and roots music, and the theatre, and is currently setting up home with his girlfriend.

T0164293

OWEN LOWERY

## *Otherwise Unchanged*

*Northern House*

CARCANET

First published in Great Britain in 2012 by
Northern House
In association with Carcanet Press Limited
Alliance House
Cross Street
Manchester M2 7AQ

www.carcanet.co.uk

A CIP catalogue record for this book is available from the British Library

ISBN 978 1 84777 200 8

The publisher acknowledges financial assistance from Arts Council England

Typeset by XL Publishing Services, Tiverton
Printed and bound in England by SRP Ltd, Exeter

# Contents

## I

## II

III

I

## *Now I'm thinking about it*

You must promise me one thing: to return
touched by the things you've seen, but otherwise
unchanged. When you bring me that other place,
that world removed, and I come to learning

the first colour you saw the sun hover
into, it must be you I'm learning through.
And when you show me the grass turning
one of the herds on the point of its hoof,

let it be the way it appeared to you,
let it come to me as the same moment,
the same instinct. Touched but unchanged, a room
the memories flicker in, but then undo

themselves from as fast when we home in
on just us again. Or will that seem new
to you as well? Perhaps I'll be the views
you first woke, the ones you'll be showing me.

## Possible first impressions

So it is, it really is, Africa.
You'll be flying from this morning inside
the passport office, the Mersey's long tide
in the yellow metal of a ticklish

sun. Your winter dreams will be colliding
with the hum and the sheen, the conviction
of a world unleashed from the restrictions
of internet photographs. As the skies

lighten and then darken again you'll feel
it tugging at you, the moment slipping
into a wall of heat, and the stars kept
waiting for your first impression, white steel

held there in the act of being chipped at
by the first blow-torch. It's then you'll unpeel
your wanting to be there, the movie-reel
taking me there as the seat-belt unclips.

## Meanwhile, back at the Chop House

There'll be an angle from which we're changed
in the jade of the Victorian tiles
every time our talking it over
finds a way between us. At that range
our thoughts lose themselves, become the smiles
the dead fill their own with. A camera
spears a moment through the evening droves
to make its own. Its wincing hammers

another into the black and white
ranks of faces we've seen, or we've heard,
or a part of us feels we should know
the difference in. In a certain light
a radio voice leaning on the words
buzzing towards us from the table
next along, could be seeing his ghost
in a mirror. His lines, made stable

for us, seem to fascinate themselves
with the prospect he's been moving from
ever since the lens came down. There's one
your son went to see with school solving
some of those enormous ifs, aloof
from the rest, more known, or more recent,
ergo larger. Their naming goes on
for several life-times in the friezes

behind the menu, with each dated
not at birth, but as they were that day
their instants found them. A busy night
told it is by the nearest waitress
swells and empties around us. We stay
as long as the wall-tiles can hold us
to our latest promises we might
return before we get much older.

## Viewing appointment at the Old Lodge

The rain had obliterated fields
and huddled trees when we last came.
Today we see how perfectly town
dilapidates. At the road's head
a municipal building is ramped and blinded
with wooden boards. Further and left
dogs are strolled on the graceful curves
of cemetery paths. Despite their stretching
the dead have yet to reach the wall,
even as their own lozenged shadows.

Passing the adjusted angles of the lodge
the black offshoots of domestic rabbits
mow a square of unclaimed land.
The road is pinched by a bridge, and will not
recover. From here on the way
is barred, forcing a u-turn in a drive
with no one looking, or else pretending.
I'm struck by the depth of the moving greens,
the balm of wood-shade, dew or moss
existing here as dominant forms.

From the outside the house is all angles.
The roof deviates from one set
of ridge-tiles to another, and the walls
are throaty pebble-dash painted beige.
The windows have been left open, all of them,
an inch or so, either for dogs,
or to prise loose a general mustiness
possibly associated with under-use,
though the latter seems less likely
for a silver hatch-back on the paved squares.

Late, but expected, so it's no surprise
when the dark wood of the front door
is just ajar. Knocking brings
to the day's edge a woman who smiles

and whose vision acquires a sense of focus
like water moving with a slight delay.
We are asked in with uncertainty
as to where we should begin, perhaps
the living-room, high-ceilinged, Edwardian red,
lit by suggestions of sunlight only.

The space, more than ample for a couple,
dwarfs the heavy timbers of chairs.
Framed kin two yards
from a blank fire freeze in acceptance,
man-handled and waiting for their next instruction.
A dining-room adjoins with the same hint
of desperation. Two dogs
recognise our difference from the patio's glass.
Are we her first viewers, I wonder?
Not quite, not really. First today though.

Hard to heat, with these high rooms?
No, she thinks not, but strains
to remember her last bill, the figures
emerging as spectral translucencies.
On her own now, her husband gone
nearly three years. Loved it,
he did, and would never have left. An impression
in the white bathroom of attrition, of lingering,
and the established theme of cool space
lit by a similar indecision.

And the bedrooms are hardly any clearer,
miscellanies and accumulations:
books and games, a huggable Womble;
two grandchildren, we're told, a chubby
boy in uniform, and a baby locked
at six months old, ungrowing.
The former has a name we fail to catch,
a regiment in Chester. The latter grins
from the limbo of his christening gown.
In the garden she thanks us both for coming.

## You with Larkin on

I can make you out
of not much light and the dark
the rain's been coming

our way from for days
now. And I can make myself
jump watching your face

so long I forget
to check your chest for moments
of breath. There, a lift

and fall of oat-meal
jumper. And again, letting
mine settle as well

once it's real. In time
with the sharp plum of his voice
clear as ice, edges

of bottles boating
the margins of trees and brief
skies. The line of lips

the rude bits make smile
a little, slips to the more
eternally you

even he'd have been
worried by. Or especially,
seeing you immune.

# Man walking

*by Stanley Park, Liverpool*

A wrap of flowers lifts him
from pavement and cemetery wall
to convergence at the point he makes
of early morning, our seeing
each other see him
at the same time, and our letting on

we have, like him, made
something of the journey to which,
in the great scheme, he's really
nothing. A man, heroic
in his middle-age, and his bearing
some of what's inside

for all the road and its morning
to see. His bouquet seems to be
spring, a reflection of the swathe
and breath of blossom, fruit
and may, ornamental
peaks of cherry dusting

the green of park, the timing
of the parked cars. A sense,
then, of destination
only wants confirming
by a fall of petal on the dark
of his back or his shoulder, a kiss

for us to remember him by.

# Morning call

Your trademark switching the light on
from the bottom end of the stairs
wakes the open secret of his
thank you prayer, and with it, the risk
you'll hear what his having you there
does for the morning, the bright sun

cutting its teeth on the latest
frost. Suddenly one of those songs
played thin on the radio you like
between the football has a spike
of truth to it, one you belong
somewhere near. It's an inflation

even the cliché must suspect
it's never deserved. But it's you
he's thanking the blue space above
the ceiling for, your name hovering
over his mouth, and with renewed
hope every time. You he elects

over the others, nurses, in-laws,
who get him all wrong, too clumsy
holding him, too conscious, making
everything real in faking it,
coming across all mumsying
like he's four again. And once you're in

he can let go, knowing this time
it won't matter. Real tenderness
just does these things without forcing
itself in on him, ignoring
the awkward stuff in defending
him as your dad from the rhymeless,

reasonless creeping up of what
just happens to us sometimes.
Weather, the light switching on, words
overheard. The simple rewards
stack up when it's your love coming
up the stairs, you for a daughter.

## Salvation Army clothes bin

Thrilling at the weight of the contact
clunking behind the bin-bags
as they tumble in, one thump
soft and heavy as a coma
for every one, and the rumble
after as the darkness comes
foaming from the tagged sins

of how many years
would that be now? years of
him to be dragged from the wardrobe
into so much space you could swim there
naked as the stars, hoarding
their dead light for the women
you could have been, off pier,

rolling the whiteness of their fire
between your breasts turned
wild again, and even more so
with the thought of the ragged men
who'll be wearing him tomorrow
down the road by staggers,
knowing how hard you've earned this.

# A spring morning's photographs

A good day for it
places against a blue sky
the degradation

of a down-spout, rust
wounds, their jags of darkness, split
between the first day

someone hammered them
into shapes of promises
meant to last, and what

they've become in time
for you to catch their gaping
reminder of work

yet to be done, ours
this time, like the window panes
the rain exposes

when it's blown across
the differences in the moors
and here, lines of cars

and curtains, the chats
with neighbours who either know
or don't how it slipped

into this morning's
snaps in the cold, the need for
truth, that proof the brief's

demanding to make
it that bit easier for us
once he's signed away

those twenty-three years
leading, stumbling, towards us
with their eyes half-closed.

# Jayne's barn owl

As if it waited on your drive
back alone on edge of our night,
suspending its stooping over
the road, its dissolving cover
into a dream expressing flight
as a completeness divided

by its sound. Around the Greyhound
was it? Or as you passed the wood
on water by the dam again?
Only once with me though, and then
I missed it, waking to the flood
of your smile and the windscreen's space

instead. The magic of it stands
against the logic of the road
being quieter then, your eyes
having room to watch the rising
of the brick farms, and your slowing
down when you drive with the strands

of one of our good days shyly
untangled. But then it must help
you've had this happen thereabouts
before, that you drive with the dare
fused, the thrill primed. It also helps
it waits there to raise its silence.

## Picturing you as a girl

With your head too big for your tiny body
tucked neatly underneath, weightless,
and a starling you've tamed perched on your finger,
there's so much of you here I know

through the blurs of the lost edges. Dark
fills the bird and your hair, the stripes
across your vest. Between there's the light
of your smile starting to laugh itself open,

but the sparks are missing from the bird. It's the shape
of itself, but in velvet, or wet coal.
How long would you say you could hold it there
before its feathers shook it from its form?

And how many other birds did you try it with
before that broken-legged survivor
got its wings? A good few
for certain, and each time you found one

clutching the same unlikely hope
they'd take to your dishes of bread and milk
without just curling under in a few days'
time, flat-eyed. Some, like the starling,

would have been injured. Others you'd pick
from the nest or the bushes and make them yours
when anyone asked, orphans, lost,
or best of all, needing to be taken

home. The same conviction screams
whenever something flies in front of the car.

## *Small tortoiseshell,* Aglais urticae

The pondside flowers just won't behave
long enough for the day's tortoiseshell
to be pinned to its mauve pediment. The picture
furs in the camera's mind, dithers
in the act, on the high-wire, of its auto-focusing,
first on a slice of green leaf, then the fuss
of petals being nibbled and played at by the wind's differences.
So many times you find the perfect
knocked from the sweet smell, aborting,
like trying to carve the moment of a wave

breaking. And it would certainly be something if we could
cup it in feathered hands and call it
September. It's been like that since we came outside though:
burning for the sun when the fringes of the clouds
catch; unrolling our sleeves again
once the heat of it lifts. A pain
when we're both reading, and you're almost proud
of your bare feet on my lap. Then it rides
over and between us, eventually falling
for one patch of colour in particular, what would be

so worth it, if you could only get the light
at an angle that doesn't just flatten it.
It'll not be for want of trying. You're on your feet,
stalking the view on which the patterns
hinge, turning the wings, the water
into the careful transfer of weight, not talking
for the moment, placing your steps in the scatterings
of paper leaves. You'll want it as neatly
as possible in the view-finder as it flicks and bats
on its flower. You'll want the image as tight,

as clean, as the lens itself, let it
slip away only once
you've no other choice but accept its loss
as a level profit. Ours anyway,

or no one's. We both know, there'll be no more
until we get another, with the sun drawing
a line beneath its presence. It's there, bending
with the flower-heads, and the image where it was,
like a sound under water, a response
the muscle in the lens is already forgetting.

# Time by Clifton Marina

An orange-tipped butterfly
winks from a shimmer of leaf
and sun, an image rich
in potential, this year's,
this spring's, linking kids

on climbing-frames, ice creams,
land once swarming with a disguising
grass. We find a place
you like, reducing their colours
to the spark on water, their sounds

like a distant train or traffic,
the more remote being heard
in a bird-sung calm. We've a lake
keeping them where they are,
a ditch on our other side

left by the canal's running dry.
Some of the thinner trees
in this part were never here.
You tell me in a way that cuts
to the seed-drop, clears

like November wind. Yes, but
having said that, what they grow from
is dead leaves, shapes
in paper. What made me think
there'd be nothing left of last

year? The bigger trees,
the ones we find faces in,
I won't say they knew you,
but you're right, they've been here more than
long enough. The 'buildings', too,

red brick, slotted
under low roofs, guarding
rubbish. A man asks us
what they mean, what they are,
accepts they could be clinging on

from the war, bunkers,
shelters? More likely remnants
of an industry long decamped,
the better for our not knowing.
Dens? Yes, sometimes,

but you were more for the branches
than anywhere else, watching,
sleeping in the filtered sun,
undemanded. Further back
where you'd struggle taking me

rabbits tore open
in your hands, wet gloves,
fetching a quid or two
from the butcher when you'd got enough.
Kids, eh? The tow-path

returns by the river, us
and couples pulling dogs.
Black daub on a bridge
says 'bridge unstable,
ha ha'. It trembles crossing,

or clicking on a statue of a heron.
Be so good, wouldn't it,
if that butterfly was still here?

## Jayne's holiday aubade

Night dives between your straining thighs.
The window's bothered me a few days.
You find the gap, Miss Practical
on your tiptoes on the Welsh bed.

Weather tears and fidgets in the stone,
scuds clouds across the recent dawn.
This was a grain barn on a cattle farm
with a baby owner in black and white

plonked on top of a working shire,
standing with his hair at his father's hip,
bright as the whitewash. Blond he was, like us,
he was happy telling us at great length

limping on a horse-kick set hard.
Your T-shirt helps, covers and not.
The window slams. No sun to speak of,
so no John Donne. But screw morning,

with you timeless in your red knickers
and the owner whistling from the barn next door.

## From Lochaline to Isle of Mull

A nothing much of a journey
with you as my gaze watching churn
and small turmoil of exchange
from the upper deck, naughty-eyed
with light and wind, an abortive
sea-weave caught and disarranged,

shaking from itself as white sparks.
You make these things remarkable
with me parked up behind steel
walls. Not the least indication
from here of the box hull breaking
waves. We're taken not feeling

the remotest change, those of us
eating in rows, or reading, bussed
from one coast to the next blind
happening. By which time you've returned
camera-happy and face burning
like a born again. Gates grind

their molars, struggle to open
a concrete pier, an empty slope
where gulls mope on hollow wings
and hollower sounds. Our next shots
should be backwards from the jetty,
with the boat just beginning.

## Stalking one of Sunart's otters

A difficult moment aside
when a wet stone has you sliding
on its riddle of golden,
almost mustard-coloured seaweed,
it's captured fairly easily,
by your pressing through the gild

with the bracts popping as you go,
by us slowing, pulling over.
How you know from the tangle
of shore-spoil, a particular
movement in the drift-wood, live rock
with a slick line, jaws fanging

a fish-chunk, gets me. But you do,
the second we leave the road too,
even showing me first, gaze
extending beyond your finger
to a point between Sunart's fringe
and its shingle. I'm dazzled

you can creep so close, following
where the sheen becomes ruptured pool.
From the yellow hem you trace
where it left you with your jeans drenched
and your view-finder still clenching
its essential displacement.

## A buzzard from Rose Cottage

In our pictures I can study
how it'll wait old-man-shouldered
with the bodies of mountains
at its back, an hour, maybe more,
silhouetted among the bare
branches, wired to that one point.

Similar but closer when caught
in binoculars, a thoughtless
presence, born to the purpose.
Could even be a candle-flame
in so far as a flame can stand
for hours bending, and then curve

to nothing. It happens once, lifts
earth on a long wing kept stiffly
to the weather as it moves
the valley. It can be followed
beneath the radar unfolding
with the rolling and rebuffs

of terrain. Croft walls and houses
hold the shadow, and then lose it.
When it closes on the bark
the world has found a new colour.
We miss the moment it re-folds
in the curled breath of pre-dark.

## Incidental composition

If we're looking for symmetry
we could do worse than these white stems,
these masts climbing from mirrors
where their other selves are gently
shattered. Their yachts are presented
incidentally, there as art

and unaffected by a sense
of being, something we mention
just the once and get used to
counting journeys, fixtures we learn
to depend on, always turning
the same corner, never loose.

They could be cenotaphs from wars
we're untouched by, though any war
might disturb that remoteness
staring from the fringe. From the hills
on the shoreline houses yellow
in the shallows, become notes

to be played on the rocks and hulls,
names for what the forest recalls
in the cold and clear. They move,
of course they do, when we're not here,
when the tide tugs at their moorings
and the deer come down in droves.

# Half-lit on a return journey

Along precisely the same route
as this morning, and colluding
with the muted sigh of light,
deer grow from the turf. By that tree
the day got brutal with, two or three
in the breezeless dusk fighting,

pretending. Some explore the dirt
by a picnic table inert,
then disturbed the way clouds are,
moving from us in their own time,
like dead relatives in a dream,
and dissembling if we stare

too hard, too long. The hills and road
are not heather, but they allude
to the truth in that colour
as a softer incarnation,
an antique pink untraceable
in the day's protracted fall

from itself. The deer carry this
with them in their fur, resisting
an insistent progression
into blue dark. It rests an hour
on the forests by Sunart's shore
between pure cold and horned flesh.

## Bill Shankly on a T-shirt

*I was made for Liverpool*
*and Liverpool was made for me,*
this in a modest white
on my lucky, my match-day T-shirt,

and on a background the colour of brick
verging on dried blood.
All right, that doesn't cut it,
not as precisely as I'd like,

but something of that honest strength,
that blind faith, thrives
in a red more grounded, more sober
than the gloss of your average replicas

named and numbered. The fact
they could have pressed onto the front
of mine any number
of these perfect epitaphs, that whispers

volumes in his gentle rasp.
I'm sure I heard it first
on a record saved from a jumble-sale
around the time the man

was dying. The funny thing was
I'd feel myself through the pops
and snaps of needle-dust,
swelling with that trapped belief,

like fields shaking with weather
which went to nothing. Like streams.
My favourites are the famous reductions
of the famous. Bobby Moore

with the gold still wet on his winning
smiled to a shadow – *Rubbish*
before the match, a crock,
a cripple on legs weak

with a night's dancing. And then,
*What a player*, re-cast
as a god with the win secured.
Or, yes, of course, the lad

he made a *monster* of, given steaks
for strength, like Joe Louis,
returning weeks on
wanting a word with the boss

and his girl-friend as pregnant as it's telling.
A more serious note. His Utopian,
his social vision. His child's
affirmation, his miner's, if you like,

working for the same goal,
sharing in the rewards. There's a statue
eight foot and near a ton
on a granite plinth. I pass

the arms like an angel's girders
with the Kop on one side,
the Church of Christ on the other,
always with my T-shirt burning.

# Andy Carroll's first Liverpool goals

*Liverpool 3 Manchester City 0*

It misses by that much, the ball
resting on the net-top, rolling
behind goal with minutes left,
and time with its head in its hands
beyond the packed moan of the stands
still demanding more from life

than the two our new man's netted
already. His first as a red
like the setting down of stones
for projected buildings, the thirst
for that feeling, and the lustre
with his first and second blown

away in their crowd moments. He
took them well, this Geordie, with teeth
like a greeting from a love
returned to years on in a dream,
(and that's so crucial, believe me),
as his team-mates came gathering

under condor arms, an Angel
uprooted from Low Fell, angled,
says the Angel's maker, just,
to give a sense of embracing.
A well-chosen celebration
and not wasted on the buzz

of that possible third hanging
for a second, then longingly
dropping, singing, and then not
quite. Still brilliant though, going home
on car radios. Another game
slips the camouflaging plot

against the same opposition
thirty years back: my first proper,
by which I mean top-flight match,
and the last hat-trick by a red
versus Man City. Dalglish bleeds
from the medley as I catch

again that glimpse between a sway
of arms, of pulses, the ball placed
in its graceful arc against
the top corner, suspended there,
as if it was really that rare,
and that perfect. With the strain

removed, the netting reshapes. No.
Not this time. Meaning each moment
keeps its own integrity.
Meaning the Angel stays guarding
its perch on the A1, staring.
Meaning words, names, can be wedged

apart. Carroll. Dalglish. Now. When.
He's off seconds before the end.
The two men shake hands, exchange
a few words, a smile, manager
to player and then back again,
with the rain on their changes

gradually becoming white stars.

# Fabrice Muamba returns

*Reebok Stadium, Bolton, 2 May 2012*

Ushered through before they can run our tickets
past the robot eyes on the wall. The speaker
rises, finding concrete to bounce the waited
moment against, lifts

forty-seven days from the dark. We make it
just in time to share in that smile the cameras
love the bones of, hands we can see suspended,
waving to forest

crowds, applauding, finding his name returning
to him carried home on the waves. His wife claps,
catching tears among the elect. A knuckle
rubs at the corners

of his eyes. For minutes on end it's not real
time. He's lost some weight, as expected maybe,
given what he's been to and back, but still stands
there in the floodlights

carving every beaming expression. Medics
shake his hand, and he, in his turn, embraces
each of theirs. A flurry of words. Also shared
knowledge of how close

darkness came to being complete. The bare facts:
seventy-eight minutes without a heart, players
praying, no one sure of their bodies, mean what,
now we can see him

blinking every second a little more true,
now your face is tumbling as well? A mascot
folds him deep in paws. He ascends the grey steps,
sits at his wife's side.

## Early morning on the ward

I return to find the white cliff
sloughed away like meringue,
the familiar paths I mind-walked
champed and smoothed by a sea

verging on lavender
with troughs of night purple, slow shapes
going dry in an hour
to leave the mollusc-eyed sand sore.

Billy is awake. I hear him
growling through the whiteness.
He takes water with a flat 'a'
and no trace of a bur.

Trish says he needs a shave
and flat-foots her way to the sink.
Her head crosses the glass
with the weightless ease of a ghost.

There are sands past the far window,
and an ambitious pier
the sea only laps to in flood.
This I learn from gossip

between sleep and washes.
There is radio noise most mornings
so today seems special.
Trish reappears, or her hair does.

She limbos beneath a devil
and a shoreline of cards
stretched across a distant bed-space
on a string. Curtains swish.

A fakir melts from rope
he's suspended from the ceiling,
stretches a lean finger
and snakes a peach from my fruit-bowl.

# In conversation with Chiron

His laughing has a wildness to it
tonight with barley wine
stripping him to National Service
and clothes the colour of the desert
somewhere past Cairo, details
fazed by the following morning

and ever since. But there are definites.
A joke rolls across the ward
lacking the needed finish,
laps the space I fill
with him, with me. Letters
hand-scrawled by his son-in-law

feature hieroglyphics,
or will. Already he's explained
finding the sound of the khamseen
in stalks of wheat, or counting
the numbers of floods or cattle,
the airy syllables in a cartouche,

is basically what keeps him here.
Young enough to be unable to think of him
any younger, this still feels like
wisdom bandy-kneed in the clear
of the Red Sea. His arms
and splinted hooves punctuate

applauded by the bent stalk
where his laughing quivers
a sand-bag paunch. There's a drunk
skill in his manipulating
his twin-handled safety mug,
his not scalding it across his lap.

One of his teachings from tonight
will concern the nature of experience
as a rite of passage, how what
we've shared is several lifetimes
stuffed into that one impact
woken from, or dived into.

# A frieze depicting four centaurs

John adores the sun with oil
plastered in nurse's handfuls on skin
brown in the way his holiday knew
diving from a boat in too little water,
grinning like a wall's fuck you.
I can never fully forget his time
for something early and awful with a hatchet,
his own non-reciprocal scars
sparking the grimace of ward glass.

Wheeled into place on his immediate right
a part of Tom has stayed a boxer
familiar with John Conteh, looking
so much like him, he could almost be him.
But it won't be confusing in a few years
when we're joined by the real one in a Toxteth
church. Between now and the funeral, the grin
and the baffled stare, the crap jokes,
will slide into an impossible slur over tins

of Guinness. A fourth, Billy, may join us
with a jug of cordial and navy rum
through a long straw. This being summer
there are always others coming round
in starched rows, learning the lie
of the ceiling's tiles. Billy in a shirt
or a jumper at all times, wants
Elvis instead of Tom Jones, the voice
of storms clotting on Saddleworth Moor.

The view from here could be plenty worse.
A girlfriend or a sister is playing tennis
moving as if her shadow doesn't know.
In a world of such small surprises,
tonight will be a goulash or a cheese salad,
the first Dirty Harry, and Bronson's
Death Wish, either One or Two.
You can tell as we lengthen across the short grass
if it isn't now it will be soon.

## Jospice visiting day

Quite a pleasant drive with the coast approaching
pines with faint suggestions, then leaning harder.
This by way of answering farms and seasons
pulsing the raw crops

where the soil has stared through the winter. Open
skies as well, the land having levelled drawing
closer. Will his voice have the strength to make it
over the low hum

always there, the susurrus breathed by machines
day on day? Conditions today are shifting
giving light to patches of road, the photo
when I arrive, found

lying shrunk in tatters in India was it?
Seems it started there, with the need as painful
in its sheer insistence as that obsessive
sun. There's a brief note

on the Jospice mission, and then an awkward
wait for clearance, seeing his eyes relearning
names and shapes. The funniest thing is never
meeting them, not once,

those he'd call his friends and his family, that is,
though there'll come a time I'll be touched to find out
what they do is come with their daily changes
after I've gone home.

When he's bright enough, we'll be sipping Guinness
just about made drinkable once Ribena
pinks the froth. Or brandy, again a pleasure
not to be dodged, not

yet, at least. A joke has me guessing longer
than it should. It rolls from his lips like treacle,
growing so its meaning becomes enormous.
Finally, words click.

Getting what it was has him sliding into
would-be laughing, more in relief. A handbag
lies beside me, which, when he sees it, has him
calling it mine. Yes.

Nodding slowly, letting the moment ripple
through him, making easy our human contact.
Driving back the evening with headlights full on
what do those sparks mean

crossing former ward-space, and winding up here?
There was boxing, something in that assessing
what it was to face an opponent head-on
maybe, the same buzz

football gives us, Liverpool red on matchdays.
Seems so fragile feeling the coast's recession
slipping over us with his drunken, stumbling
grimace, his weak joke.

## Hospital slide-show

When they come for the nurse she does not exist.
She's born where light smears the wall
of what we know to be a hospital ward.

Is this the first time I see the dead?
I keep the colours, just in case.
There are the quills of a deep grassy sea

hot with blood, and a uniform's white
in certain places. We met by accident
on a train, or reading somewhere else

not entirely in our own thoughts.
Not for long enough to really know
the wide open of the eyes as more

than a smashed mirror, epiphany's stopped
now. Otherwise it's so much worse
than a stillbirth. She's soundless, processed

like the gunner of the ball turret, and yes
they may well hose her from the green
presumed to be spreading beyond the glass,

those who took her with a gun that is
and for whom she lies with careless knees.

## IVP – *intravenous pyelogram*

Does this qualify as perfusion?
There is movement at the foot of the table
that I know relates to an injection,
dye into one of the veins
in one of my feet, completed
with a delicate Indian courtesy,
thanking me for what exactly?

The giving, the yielding, is the vein's.
Enforced patience could not
be easier unless it were the nerveless
inspection of the collimator,
passing up and through the abdomen,
the aperture winking when it's done,
set to repeat, reconfirm.

There's time between assessments
for *Goodbye to All That*,
Challoner as war's rumour,
briefly at a billet's window,
his fatal wound from Festubert
presumably interred somewhere
and his cap-badge immaculate.

Not him as such, but the means
of seeing and recording, the vapid,
the otherwise unseeable. He was there,
Graves says, with his regiment
miles down the line, adrift.
Your fingers find my temples
drawing their small circles.

These do not appear as mist
sculpted on a series of black
screens, bones under water,
milky swirls of star-birth.
Soon, a man we've never met
will place his hand on my shoulder,
stare deep and tell me

Jesus loves me. It will happen
between the bread and the cheese sellers
of a market here for the weekend.
In a week the hospital will have written.
The collimator hums
as you and the doctor shelter
behind a glass breakwater.

II

## Quinming at Noyelles-sur-Mer

With spring and an eastern sun
porcelain settles on rows
of stone. She will come bearing
branches flared with the grey flows

of willow, a jug of wine
from the Nanwang valley
based on what a grandparent said
of his dead father. He shall

know again the bitter tang
and smile like the photographs
can only imagine. Time
awards a name and the rote

parade of open landscape
where he slopes to nothing. Love,
they say, gives greater meaning
to this green season. When she moves

she will know how the caution
of the man she honours stepped
between ranks of red flowers
and the sourness of the ripe

mud. Her one, she has learned, died
as he tried to tame a duff
shell. For others also marked
with a stark number, the coughs

rattled Maxims in their lungs,
or they clung to a shell-hole
not quite safe from the bullets'
song. Billeted in sallow

camps, they'd maybe share their girls,
passing curled images round
their bored confinement. The rains
would have been nothing new, sounds

of grain scattered on baked soil,
grabbing shelter for a while
under waterfall pagodas,
tin sheet just about bullied

into basic roofs. The gate
the cemetery cries behind
is rather nice, a calming
remote dignity, and blind

almost to the nearest town.
Out of bounds to him, more lost
than China, and steering clear
of the yards where they'd cluster

and talk unknowably. France
as distance. France as flattened,
or ruptured and needing soil,
needing coolies. She will pat

the lions on leaving, gifts
from the afterlife of new
China, new or rebuilt France.
One more glance, and return through

the sun to her flat in Paris.

## Wilfred Owen by the canal at Ors

*November, 1918*

From this side the canal is a steel sheet,
occasionally ruffled by the breezes
that can turn skin to stone in the whiteness
of a second. A painter tries to tease
life into trees in an otherwise void
scene, with infinite attention to form
and November's skittish light. Its bite bloods
the rims of his eyes, pinches his hands numb.

A week more, and none of this would matter
in the least, he could save it for the sun
and the stench of life in the capital,
or file quietly past the monuments
with the rest, wreath in hand, and the feeling
that part of him was left here by the cut.

# Unmarked war dead at Fromelles

## 1916–2009

There are great plans for a space like this
pinning down the dew of men,
drooling in a porridge of wet cement
the hollows and constrictions of names and numbers
their photographed shadows were always known by.

They will be touchingly re-fleshed and re-attached
with the black veneer they've successfully acquired,
the presumed leaf-mould of time's camouflage,
unpeeled. Similar out-survives
at the limits of car parks and school fields

the first mêlées of the year's snow,
a hundred or so if you want the count.
This copse of theirs is well-mannered
and the flat fertility of the enclosing land
neatly ploughed and planted over.

To buddy the rolling of particular seasons
cars can be heard purring through the trees
from the confines of a toy road, though less
in summer. The bracken can be quite discreet
though the tree canopies tend to whisper.

It's not all homogeneous sludge.
With patience a language of brass buttons,
the former silver of a gentleman's watch,
presents itself for debriefing. Letters
require perhaps greater patience,

gaps or tears or burns have to be filled
with conjecture. This much we do know:
whoever owned this smutted Bible
was rather fond of the book of Romans,
judging, that is, by his underscorings.

Whereas the next item initially repulses.
The wet leather is too clumsily organic
and for a second you doubt the natural process
to scour clean and announce the bone.
You remember a burst man is damp and red,

and forget as finite inspection says
this is actually a heart his lover has traced,
cut out, and stitched together.
Inside, the torn pieces of a note
refuse to co-operate with a lock of hair.

## Frost and Edward Thomas walking

*Near Ledington*

The words were the least significant aspect
shouted or sung across an expanse
of hawthorn by way of greeting, a shared
acknowledgement rooted firmly in being
part of the changing season. It stuck
with one of the men who took to the lane
that evening, who talked the end of the summer
down. And was that defined in the voice
which spotted their passing there, and which called
a halt to their strolling rhythm? The friends
were always on walks that summer the war
was waiting on, making rich what was left
before they were both away, to the front
for one, or to holing up on his backwoods
farm for the other, drawing apart
like halves of a shell. Perhaps it was more
that feeling of closure hemming them both in,
making the moment sharper, than what
the American called the *cadence* of greeting,
not that it hadn't lodged in his thinking.
Pushing a pitchfork through an unsettled
outline of hay, a type, or a landscape
moving despite himself, was the man
who'd shouted them. Day, or maybe the weather,
stole what he said. The sound of it hung,
but hollowed away, a flint being struck,
the weight in the distant rolling of bells
between their exchange and Ledington proper,
now, and a moment shaking the ground
to pieces of mud and memory at Arras.

## For Helen Thomas

How to catch those hesitations
mistaking easterlies in the ash grove,
the hearth, the row of bean-canes,
breathing them the first tickle of sweat

from the station, his easy march uphill
the soot-plumes gradually obscured,
his half-whistle and half-song
reversing its decline from a wet morning,

the throwing off of the cap, the fingers in hair
and the cut chill of brass buttons
feeling just a little ridiculous
in the draught, dressless in the clock-glass,

gawky as a fairground mirror, laughing
and not altogether knowing why,
the way you do when it's been a while
and you're stood there once more open-handed.

## Outskirts of Ypres, 1920

*based on an account by Stephen Graham*

Past the bugle and the Menin Road
a couple with tactile and inquiring lips
lose themselves and are lost to the general
fug: tobacco and conversation,

to which they resemble twinned trees,
ironwork blasted into new conjunction
broken with the spikes of their seminal rails.

A waitress, a girl at any rate,
tells a man with a medal and a wall-eye
she is not for sale, she is no man's
and never an Englishman's – they lie, always.

He admires her ghost in the spilt wine
pooling across the table, redness curling
and clinging to the base of his fingered glass.

For another at the same table, offhand,
something about knowing where the soldiers are,
if he likes, if he'll follow her a little way
but not please for jig-a-jig.

A drift all evening under an obscured clock.
Clientele and the mist: yellows, ochres,
lighter and deeper by diurnal turns,

a touch warmer or cooler in a street
of barred doors and vacant barrows.
Levering, clambering over rubble, softening
to the tremor of an eyelid otherwise asleep.

A crash and star-fall of dumped munitions.
The peculiar colorations of the dead.

# A day's work with Kitty Blake, 1937

Thirty-two by now with her line perfected,
firstly down at Hadley's, the master himself
cultivating grapes you'd have sworn were swelling
clear of the white glaze,

then at Worcester's having the girls in stitches,
part of what they knew as the Saucy Sestet.
Time has time for her with the painting over,
tea in the canteen

cooling just enough. It's a bramble morning,
was a bramble one, if she's being fussy.
Light's the thing with blackberries. Curve the light round
each of the nodules

then the latest crop should just finish themselves.
When it's grapes, she needs to remember Hadley
skating gentle colour across the wet globes,
love like a surgeon's

bending closer, giving his brush the chance to
flow. Her lips attach a remote and red kiss
where her cup begins. It's a proper trademark
that is, then laughing

not a bit embarrassed. With time to spare, just,
meaning one more cigarette gets the same stain.
Soon the autumn leaves will be burning orange
touched with the white veins

needing finer brushes. Another forte
when you know your stuff like our Kitty seems to.
But the wireless helps, or it does when Adolf
isn't the day's news,

when the bands are on and she nearly forgets
letting instinct manage the final image.
Signing off, she'll leave it to drying after
hoping it stops there.

## Jasmine tea at a pavement café

*from Keith Douglas's* Alamein to Zem Zem

An afternoon to dream the guns
to wisps of cloud from Tel Aviv,
an interplay of light and shade
over textured stone, serves to give

precision to a moment, cuts
arrangements of pavement tables
in the white flags themselves. And him
with them, stretching from the stable

core of his recovering flesh
with a newspaper browsed away
to obituaries, an upbeat
scoop from the sands of Alamein.

Jasmine tea, a taste picked up
in Cairo, revisits a girl
and her lover, keen-eyed with smiles
locked in photographs and a world

of dust between them. Now a name
to parade on her skilful tongue,
shuffle and replace with a lad
still out there somewhere, or wrongly

supposed. His darkness nearly told
until he caught it by the mane,
opted for the easy mirage
in *maybe* and something painless

on red pillows. Her hair swirling
and dispersing inside the cup
spins the same overwhelming scent.
Her barter and low *Yes* ripple

in the murmur of slow traffic,
talk from assemblies of young men
dressed in the desert and the sun,
women happy knowing again

where the tan ends, offering thanks
to the dunes for their coin. Or no,
that was night in another town
somewhere in his unguarded groan,

a time well outside the remit
of what the black print hammers down.

## Keith Douglas painting dancers

The lads at bayonet practice
have been replaced. Between the cracked
plaster, their packs are removed
and laid upon an arena
of eggshell blue, almost serene,
with the green of their dead youth.

They rise from themselves, uncoiling,
flexing into shape from the soil,
each a small miracle. Flutes
can be heard in their rehearsals
where their yesterday is dispersed
and night bursts through. An astute

observer will already know
as their movements come to a slow
and remote recognition.
Their characters, such as they are,
are not unfamiliar, but stars
grow aware of their new flesh

and colour them accordingly.
They seem immune to the orders
of their former painter, much
to his amusement. Reds implode
in favour of a soft bleeding
into steady silvers, sucked

into a separate state. Their change
exceeds his preferred arrangement,
and their strangeness. His study
at Christ's Hospital tied them down,
planted them in columns, the sounds
of drill pounding in their blood.

Palestine better becomes them.
Here, in his billet, they have bloomed,
a consummation of sorts,
their eyes reflecting smashed mirrors,
their minds freed from their birth's terror.
Who they were is dried water.

# Shalimar Gardens, Lahore, 1943

*based on the letters of Alun Lewis*

Replacing embers of dark robins
collecting thinly on the garden walls
by first light, light yet to be bugled
to high day, a brown soutane
and a white beard, a pair of specs
made natural by a dab of sun,
like he's been recently touched by Renoir
and left drying where the shade snaps.

A masked smile, the stillness and movement
of water, greet him among the terraces
with an extended hand, reassuring
that the elements have agreed their mutual terms.

Among the privacy of the parched trees,
Lahore seeming otherwise deserted,
he's almost obliged to be the first to talk,
semi-fluent in valleys' French.

Wales, he says, is a green land,
Cwmaman village dark and small,
made smaller still by the soaring hills,
and does the priest ache for *his* home?
and what is the difference between God and war?
one reflection to another, the priest to the soldier,
the calm of Shalimar, the smooth water,
*My son, you lack our consolations.*

## On deck with the secret sleeper

*based on the letters of Alun Lewis*

A vast expiration of lucid stars
new and uncluttered by light's noise, ageless
by his terms, quivers darkly above him,
unfolds a languid arm, a cold caress.

His subconscious voice succumbs, relaxes,
absorbs the slow percussion of the sea,
the warm thrum of turbines, plate steel clenching,
the night gushing its refreshing sweetness.

He'll whisper as much in his letters home
and immerse in his old familiar pain,
knowingly and deliberately confuse
Cwmaman's heavy hills with the contours

of each undiscovered land. Faces blend
degrees of separation. A brown girl
flexes by a brothel wrapped in Welsh vowels,
the New World's eyes stare whiteness from the mines

and the tireless pit-wheels of his dreaming.
He'll save his last thought for the flimsy deck.
He'll let the rancid stink of the troopship
slip quietly through his fingers, his secret

guarded by the round hull of a lifeboat.
It's conceivable he *was* felt soft-shoed
and in shorts passing through the sleeping men
to lie stripped above, turn grey with the moon,

if not by the lads triple-tiered in bunks,
then by the ancient hand of the spectre
who shakes him to himself in the morning
to douse the place he lay with clean water.

## Random encounters, Cwmaman

Pure enough to look at, but rank,
a drain-smell escaping the banks
and the spanked out plants clinging
to the gleam of what the town was.
Still the belief he might've lost
minutes, glossy and singing

something remotely Welsh in light
weakening into dusk. His polite
glance inviting, suggesting,
not company, though alive
to the possibility, but life
itself, shivered into, guessed

towards on the surrounding hills
where crows fidget through the stillness
on the coal. Filled with the void
themselves, they squabble over holds
on the chimneys, an unfolding
he's seen spoiled with the destroyed

lungs of the old ones who always
wash indoors. Washed. I should say
washed. A grey terrace opens
and a man, youngish, with a smile
like bad milk and a strange mildness,
asks me why I'm here, too slow

to be hostile, *just asking, see?*
I tell him we're here for pieces,
the unseen world of Lewis.
*The poet?* Yes, the poet, born
here, died Burma, himself yawning.
*You know more than me. Been a few*

*here for him though.* We get strong tea
in tin mugs, and a DVD
with the greenness bleached from trees
bristling between the quiet mines,
more than a hint of him winding
down and finding his own peace

by accident. *A machine tore
my finger off. Look. Blood pouring
everywhere there was. Don't work
now. I prefers just being here,
seeing what sorts of people appear.
Spent five years at that school, there.*

Not there in fact, as much rubble
as school, with rusted wheels and scrub
for the hubbub where he played.
I take pictures, as if it helps,
the streamlet, and a young couple
as a sculpture where he bathed.

# Canto waiting for soup

*from Primo Levi's* If This Is a Man

All this in an hour of waiting for their soup
passes between a pair of what remain men
setting themselves aside from their stooping

companions, partly by the space they engender
between them, something verging on abstraction,
but also tethered to the constant sense

of practical need these places subtract to
once the memory of what they were has faded
from the hard bone. Though even the interaction

the two men engage in begins from, is made
partly from, a need to teach one of them how
to speak Italian. They'll start with words they say

all the time, the things which can be pointed out
and laid a hand on, eaten, or else stolen
and then eaten, but less openly, the *now*

which stretches so far, like a river swollen
by a long winter the banks of which collapse
under the strain, a black river unfolding

over the past and the future and lapping
against the sides of any trace of landscape
they might remember, flooding the smallest gaps

a face in a doorway, the weight of a hand,
might otherwise shine from. They're carried from there
to Dante, the Teller finding it in strands,

pulling them apart, feeding them carefully
to his Listener, beginning with the poet
finding Ulysses in a talking flame shared

with Diomed, the point of the flame glowing
and reshaping in time with Ulysses's words.
An image, a pattern, begins to grow from

the first metaphor as the men get herded
through their world of work, the shadows of barbed wire
crossing the edges, the odd blink of a world

outside them so easily lost with its spires
and its wooded towns, lost with so much the one
with Dante on his dry tongue has seen expire,

ghosted away. Just the embers where it shone
in his youth. Not that they're older here, as such,
so much as eroded. But he must go on

once he's started, rejoining after he's touched
the part about Penelope's ancient faith
in Ulysses's image. And his, not much less,

but seduced by the vastness tugging at waves
of open sea. Just that returns, the great sea
itself, turning over and over, wet caves

smashing their heads apart, salt mouths releasing
and regaining hold on their brief solidity:
an idea both of the men can feel teasing

their routine, their living at the beck and call,
the yelp poised on the metal taste of whistles
capable of wrenching a man from his soul

in the one blast, there like a jagged blister
the mind keeps stepping on. Yet dissipated
by what the Teller offers up as a gift

to his Listener, something stronger than waiting
to see whether the waters will come for them
of their own accord, something more elated

in its embracing what exists past the dumb-
as-tombstones standing there on someone's order;
an active word breaking from the drummed in

and actually, actively, just *setting forth*
instead, a concept the Listener finds himself
more than able, more than ready to support

having sailed himself, he says. So he's a wealth
of such sweet hours of his own he can call on
to help the words come across an unhelpful

break as they're pushed by. Even so, it all falls
into place now, this notion of their being
able to step outside the wire, climb the walls

with the guards and the kapos dulled by seeing
too much of the same eternity that keeps
the two men talking. One's ignoring the scene

change of a different cloud passing in its sleep.
The Listener's sucking nutrition from the lines
the first gives him at least a peephole into,

aware all the time of the sun's rising sign
wearing out their one hour together before
the soup's ready to be carted out on time.

Time they've got no claim on, time in cold storage,
time frozen like a hand on a length of steel
wanting more than a thin light from the morning

sun. And then the rhymes gum on his tongue, feeling
wrong somehow, not fitting the way they should do.
Until the speech, until Ulysses appeals

to something those who've gone that far with him hold
inside them, have buried in the distances
gazing from blank eyes they hardly acknowledge

his shape against the sun with, unresisting
the path that's brought them so far from the memories
of what was real, the words they have for histories.

It's this point the Teller's lost mountains stem from
moving freely between Milan and Turin
on a train, on a train's fluid resemblance

to the past it must have taken him through more
times than enough. And back to the broken crew
faced with a mountain of their own, a forward

pressure as the stink of the soup hangs its dew
over the final minutes of their journey.
The Teller's clawing at the last, the last few

tercets, the whole point. The remnant he's turning
over on its stave, trying to work towards,
glimmers when the sun hits a wave. A burning

need to get it just right starts edging forward
on the sores of his wooden shoes, that shuffle
he's learnt as defence against the remorseless

diurnal rhythm trodden out by the life's
worth of a pit-horse, the towering endlessness
of days meant to be exactly as bereft

as this might not be if the lines can be pinned
to the moment of their meaning. If only.
If there wasn't the soup under its wet skin,

the cough of the punctual wakening to its own
overbearing importance, drawing them in.
That, precisely that, makes an inverted cone

of water beneath Ulysses and his men,
tipping the wood of their boat at the skyline,
pulling the whole lot down into eventual

absence, leaving them choking on the saline.
New words test themselves against finality
announcing the soup, striking at the nail-head

with an iron hammer. The banality
of it all sloshes in the bowls before them.
The Teller holds his Listener back, a stalling

the words he's after answer by reforming.
*And over our heads the hollow seas closed up.*
There's hope the Listener finds in his exhorting,

the same sense of it as a way of growing
out from the visible shell of the general
humanity gulping it down in grey rows.

*Kraut und Rüben. Kraut und Rüben* extending
into the day before and the days to come
in a single identical dimension.

The voice of Ulysses at last succumbs to
the hell-flame the poet bound him in, his boat
a mess of matchwood for the sea's slow tumbling.

The Listener knows enough now to stay afloat:
the Italian for looking as far beyond
as the vision allows, the word for *remote*

surviving the latest line-up for the once
a day of the soup-call, and the chunk of bread
they get, even what it means to have wandered

so far on the Teller's breath, to be led there.

# Remember Steinlauf

*based on* If This Is a Man


Scrubbing at his scrawn without soap
and the coal set to cover him.
The word 'frivolous' occurs, moves
away though, questioning its own

pertinence. Old Steinlauf must know
washing that way, it cools you down,
it works at the man inside, drowns
him if he's not careful, turns blue

beneath the sallow. He'll not stop,
doesn't matter what anyone
tells him, they're just trying to mend
a hole in the fog. He'll not stop,

this or the other side. It's this
keeps him wired to his own routine
inside routine. A soldier's boot,
before the clogs stomped him blisters,

commands itself to walk that bit
taller than the wooden shuffle.
You pick your feet up, you have to
out-do, out-work. His hard-bitten

smile comes over, scuffing the skin
with the jacket he's been holding
safe between his knees, then hauls it
back on. Simple as good and sin,

chess-piece vision cut from the Alps
before they caved in. But it works,
it works for him. One miracle
bears another, and it all helps.

# Lilith of Camp Buna, Auschwitz, 1944

*based on* If This Is a Man

We must imagine the pattern of a war
unravelling bombs from a flakless sky,
guns not even bothering with the arc
needed to trace where they plough across
drowsing like summer bees. West.
They move West, losing themselves
from the sun rising behind their bubble
glass. Of the two men we find
pressing their bellies in the mire, one
is sufficiently clear-headed to keep it
sharp, the impact, the taking cover
in whatever form it comes to hand,
metal pipe, a ditch they dug
between them, before events kicked them
from the dirt, having left them there
as long as the numbers on their right arms.
The man he crouches with has a name:
Tischler, meaning carpenter. This too
he records. The latter speaks better
in the tongue he doesn't try to share
with the one we're indebted to. Enough
passes between them to discuss a girl
hunched in the earth somewhere close,
humming the remoteness of a folk song
rocking her shoulders to its other time,
stopping only to mend her hair. And an apple
Tischler pulls from the hunger they all of them
wear beneath their eyes and their cheek-bones.
But this happens before the girl, because
for both of the men this could be their birthday;
they could both be twenty-five. She'd be
younger, or she always was. Lilith
Tischler calls her, at which point we know
more than the man who at first believes him.
Lilith, the first woman, Lilith,
who told Adam where to go,

who wanders the void in constant need.
Their first apple it was, for a whole year.

# Shulamith at last by the River Seine

*from Paul Celan's 'Death Fugue'*

Ashen curls in the darkness of the waters
beneath the day. A woman is beginning
to walk away, to walk away
moving freely with the drowsed river,
moving among the backward clouds.
Flattered by the sudden difference of the light

on her tumbled shoulders, she moves the light
in her ashen hair. Her shadow makes the waters
before the moment of her song clouds
behind her. It was her only song in the beginning
when she kissed with a king on a distant river.
It's only song as she fades away

trailing her name. Once away
the music in the water and the music in the light
orchestrate her memory for the river.
A man she knew is watching how the waters
close around her. A man's beginning
to lose her in the ashen curls of the clouds,

to have her replaced by the same clouds,
to have her, and to let her pull away
on a smoke-string, to flicker her beginning
in the cold of a wet flame, the light
shattered and divided among the waters.
And after her comes the music of the river.

If she saw him as he chose the river
the vision will be hers, hers through the clouds,
hers among the gauloises where the wine waters
the talk of lovers, the cafés away
from his stepping in. Swallowed with the clouds
he clings to the spark of their time beginning

over. She was never ashen in the beginning.
She was seed-cake and honey with a king from a river.
She was the song they shared, a light,
a lover's song. She danced in the clouds,
he remembers that. She danced away
on the frozen wind. Her shadow made the waters

shine. Her hair only turned as the clouds
blotted and fell so softly away
from their beginnings, from light on the river, from the waters.

# Exit Leon

*from Piotr Rawicz's* Blood from the Sky

A goat to be tamed, to nuzzle the hand
as warm and alive as wounding. The lawyer,
Leon, is given words that seem so much
bigger than his or anyone's mouth,
an image for suffering straight from a text
the synagogues dried to nothing as long
ago as the oldest photographs stretching
albums and families back to their first,
their fountainheads. Leaders' words, or an actor's
waiting on death, at once both concealed
and seen as it homes in. Weighted with poignant
reference to how his audience, the two
who might have 'survivor' written inside
their blood, should regard their lives as a precious
witness, and how estranged from themselves
they'll be in the time they've left to become
a part of the world again. And apart,
both life, and its echo. Speaking to let
the words and their impact settle between them,
age and experience turn to the future
knowing that boots are coming to take
and burn and extinguish. There, in the space
between them, the couple sit down and listen
harder than guns and walls to the goat,
the metaphor sucking heat from the lawyer's
fingers. Naomi, Boris, a ghetto
soon to be ripped to picture-frames. Toys,
and suitcases. Boris there as a portal
through which the lawyer's speech can extend
towards, and encompass us. Then the human
detail of stillness snaps with Naomi
picking the *Magen David* from jackets,
outfits for she and Boris to wear
once Leon gets led away from the scene
with milk on his fingers, trailing his words.

## Treblinka's trees

*from Lanzmann's* Shoah

By no means to be seen as eugenic
metaphor, for all they were set to fail
or grow at the same moment, and despite
the vagaries making some of them stand
firmer and taller, while the frailer trees
fold over. The fact is, covering
mattered more than the business of excusing
as the time flexed, finally, the forests
fell further and further behind them,
blinding the spaces to reminders of their waste,
preserving what they'll tell you, all of them, was always
such a peaceful place you'd picnic here,
spend the night blending with the slight
disturbances of the wind turning in the wood,
the sounds you only seem to hear
after absences, after the vast
silences, miles on the midnight rails
under the eyes of the stunned and the stupefied,
the farmers, let's face it, who'd be familiar
with at least part of that logistical process
by which this or that one's weeded out
sooner or later. In the sun their straightness
shimmers, their bark climbs the darkness
pervading decades from the fact. They've fattened
from the rush of needing to push a screen
across, of course, from an order herded
through an afterthought, grafted
on a circumstance. A confirming, a disguise rising
above itself, hovering in the breath
expended there. Or is that our tendency
to want this to be a more haunting scene
than it already is, the dead's insistence?

## Die Mörder sind unter uns – 1946

*loosely based on a film by Wolfgang Staudte*

Cities in monochrome need no adjustment,
but is this truly a city in the strictest sense?
It isn't just the trick of expressionist
lighting. The odd vertical structures,
such as they are, long for the comfort
of a new word. *Buildings* sounds hollow,
the tinsel flakes of falling glass.

Faces are selected from the rubble by virtue
of their slight difference, but they are all of them degrees
of the same darkness. Pasts emerge
but lack conviction. In one of the few
streets left intact, Susanne
shares living-room with a surgeon, name of
Mertens. She stepped from a cattle-truck

where the line ends and from blurred origins.
That, though, is all we get, plus the simple
act of loving. There's no asking
how when the clocks say Zero Hour,
*Stunde Null.* You feel the rubble knows,
sentient, amorphous, without direction
or the gift of speech, like Mertens after one

too many. If Susanne is love,
the surgeon's guilt. Why else would he lead
like a broken smile, the businessman Brückner?
a man who'd sell helmets to the headless,
and recognised in an instant by his former underling.
Mertens picks his way across oblivion
and what he knows now must be done.

Nothing's secret in a ruptured world.
There are numbers among the stone scales
corresponding to a row of dead weights,
an account of Polish hostages to be balanced
out. Brückner is so good with figures,
always was. It was Christmas Eve,
for Christ's sake, and some were kids.

Brückner stumbles across himself
behind the two friends who've learned to walk
like wild dogs. It helps that Susanne
has flat shoes and Mertens has kept
his Wehrmacht boots. Sometimes her hand
moves to his, brushes with its shadow.
Mertens's hand is a clenched stump.
It must be the horrors, drinker's hells.

City shoes are useless here.
Even when they find a paved stretch
Brückner slips on a polished sole
and is yanked up. The camera's ready
for a vital zoom. Mertens halts,
fumbles the murder in his coat pocket.
Here is as good a place as any.

# Mural of Annette McGavigan

An automatic eyes the ground
snapped just below the barrel.
This frames another *Guernica*
of angles clattered down

and like searchlights reaching for the space,
the air they left dazzled,
a theatre of pigeon wings.
You can decipher odd details

from collision, angles torn
from the real. But why, when a butterfly
like none you've seen can hover
like sliced jungle, mauve,

a bruised colour to be adored
for the blurred traces of beginning.
The girl herself is gauche,
teenage-clumsy in her blouse,

stocky, and smiling, uniform
pristine giving the impression
of a new purchase for the school year,
of someone the butterfly could settle on

until shaken or blown loose.

## Unveiling of the Omagh memorial

An early closing of shop-fronts
the grey length of Market Street
refracts and distorts in fused glass,

laminations forced together
and cupping now, the open wound,
the Fibonacci staircase of a heart.

Here, you want to believe, want
like an aching womb, essence climbs
from flags and wet petals

strewn half-consciously by kids
subdued by intuition, or fed up
in the rain. Umbrellas file away

from the green of the Strule's garden,
collapse to the sound of pigeon-wings
and flow quietly through a town

made famous in a second by silence,
shock-wave. The order by which they came
shrivels; the physical ripple of lament

and the day's late prayers. It's a heavy
sunless day that stares
from the garden pool, so when they pass,

their shapes cast vague impressions
you can't distinguish from the trees.
The stage, where dignitaries gathered,

remains in black cloth. Standing
by the pond, thirty-one mirrors, in all,
wait to flood the town's heart

with sunlight reflected from a gable.

## Domodedovo airport, 24–1–2011

*for Anna Yablonskaya*

An instant flowering of a sun
develops over several frames,
a white need at the centre
you can't pin to any
one person in particular,

to shadows gathered in a lobby
waiting on arrivals, a face
worked or lived with suddenly
unfamiliar, a star,
the dreamt matter rising

in nocturnal water, crossed
by a system of eccentric ripples
drooping them on stacks of luggage,
benches on the rather perfect
repetition of the marble floor,

sculptures under circles of dust
as shy and elusive as the sense
of what, what happened here
clanging deep inside the ear,
our capacity to understand

by any other method
than pointing the exact second
on a replay, the disappearing
hereafter, a melting away,
a burning off even of their shadows.

# In a market town they're discussing him

*on the death of Osama bin Laden*

In the market talk is of how this man
in a basic room with his back towards
the spectating world is in fact a neighbour,
one fetched and carried for, tamed, run cold

with his age. The news has him watching, curled
in a shawl, the words he rehearsed exploding
like petals cast in the reddened dust.
But his beard is perfectly black on screen.

And the screen itself is a boxy portable
twenty years off its prime. The walls
are the colour sand can become, once clouds
bring the mountains close with their bitter metal.

A simple turban does little hiding
his whiter hair. In his hand the power
remains to turn himself up, or switch
himself off for good, and the speech his finger

explains to microphone stems, and canvas
it looks like, draped in a way that could be
a campsite anywhere. Heads are shaken.
This man? The one in the paper? No.

That's a no one. Ask if you want, they'll tell you.
A ghost, you know, like in any town.

## Poster at a bus shelter – Brynn

Unremembered words from the British Legion.
As a poster it's only a partial success
protected by the glass display panel
where shell-suits wait, but not for buses,
bone-faced, blank-eyed, each with an agenda
of its own inside the group dynamic.
                        One peers
against a car window. Another plants a firework
in the mouth of a post-box, lights it, runs off.
Anything it seems to kill the cold.

The poster gets ignored, either seen before
or becoming the yawn of public art.
The exploding firework applauds itself.

One side of the face, the left,
is undamaged, from which we can make
a young man, an eye, the flexing
of a top lip over white teeth.

There's more than a hint of uniform, beige,
the presumed colour of foreign dust.
What mostly reaches across the raw night
is the pressing to the other side of the forehead
of a dressing,
                        blood in a dark slick
from which the right eye is half closed.

III

## Boats at a Tutankhamun exhibition

These we could imagine out of matchsticks
slaying years by an absorptive process
to be tallied on prison fingers, and knowing
it matters only in the way a dream
or a memory does. A child could love them
in a different world, or in this as they shove
from rushes to find the seamless shimmy
of the king of rivers, puzzle how the flow
holds them, deciding while carried by the slowness,
like kindle blown before the cotton catches.

We've pictures, all of us, of boats like these,
an early currency like cave art,
not innate, but there in a different way.
Hulls the shape of a drawn bow.
Cabins mounted at one end,
or somewhere near the middle, and depending
on the day's conditions, smoke going
towards the sea's edge in a crayon grey
from which the paper label has to be peeled apart.
Always on the same stuck seas.

When they move is it under their own volition
on water purely as reflections, wakeless,
pictures again? Or is the will that poles them
on their quiet journeys his, the boy
with the gold face and eyes in obsidian,
the skull-hole punched out as a lasting riddle
for amateur sleuthing? It's certainly his enjoyment
behind the gold throne sitting on the solar
and lunar barques with a perfect take on
the sky's river, the stars' unrolling.

Not the boats as their model selves, of course,
but real, large-scale, transformed by their crossing
of that unilateral membrane between worlds lying
one on top of the other, the flexing,

tweaking, beginning. It's here we start
to lose them, that point they slip from port
and their public spectacle. It's the calm defection
of the riverside crocs on the long glide,
leaving to the daylight their last impressions,
the same transferring of dumb force.

## The boxer of Quirinal

Along with what had seemed an unrelated piece
they found his muscled body given careful rest,
a friend's, or lover's. This was no rushed unseating
of any old unneeded god. They took their best,
their most important cloth to wrap the parts, and laid
them where they must have known, in time, they'd get to rise
like grain, be put together. Turning half away,
the bearded face inquires, or looks, at least, the shade
of having seen a neighbour about him, surprised,
or just assessing who it was who came that day

to watch him fight. Or waiting jurisdiction, tense,
but giving off the blasé seen-it-all-before
of poker stars, the veterans of battles who sense
the rawness welling up in new recruits, their words
just spilling over. Winning, that would help, but not
so much you let it show. The same goes for the pain
inlaid as copper scars around the forehead, lips,
eyebrows, and dripping down the chest and thighs. They'll clot
before he's due to wind his knuckles in those strips
of dead leather, flex his centuries of training

until the bindings creak like cart-wheels, yet again.
He's punched so many times his weight in millet-sacks
the stench of bread just makes him sick these days. In plain
unpatterned speech, he'll tell you, as his fingers crack
the flesh from a dried fish, he'll never quit, not now
it's gouged so deep a scar. He's what they call the stone
soul of the old Palaestra, part of its fabric.
They'll have to bury him there, that's what, his split frown
and all. He's not averse to girls, the ones who comb
those parts of town where his blending in's a habit,

a stoop. Did he say he'd fought for nobles, you know,
like they did for old Patroclus? Left to his sweet
devices, sitting there, he doesn't mind who slows
from what they're doing, who reaches down, to greet him,
or rub his left hand, for luck, or for touching's sake.
They'll have a guess, of course, unpeeling him from strips
of good cloth. And in seeing how his hand's been worn
compared to those colossal muscles, and the breaks
his cheek-bones show, the copper inlay bleeding drips
like resin beads, they'll edge towards the word *adored*.

# Café table Sapphic

Often sitting still at her favourite table
staring tides away, and then returned, gentle
breezes making movement of sculpted hairline,
testing her red wine.

What she does depends. There are days it's simple
taking warmth and letting her lips enliven
blushed and fed by goblets to linger over.
Otherwise writing

seems enough, her pen on a scrap of paper
keeping pace with sea-lit equations, bird-calls.
Waiters give her distance on these intense days,
kindness she's paid for.

Time's become an art since the man who carried
people every day from the harbour's slipway
loved her there. It wasn't like that in all truth,
but there are rumours

and, when gossip starts, it can get adhesive.
Whether what she looks for can be located
hardly matters. Nor if the lucky object
happens to ferry

life, or colour's purity, where the water
changes hands with air in the dazzled breakers.
Men and girls have come and have sat beside her.
Some have bequeathed her

fragment voices which, to the distant music
ushered shoreward, play in her mind like blossom
honed to one perfected example, brilliant,
chosen by sunlight.

Once the waiter heard, or he could have misheard,
she'd a daughter somewhere, a Cleo? Cleïs?
Ask yourself then. But, for some reason, who knows,
people get awkward

once it comes to facing her. Breeding lends her
status which, in turn, has this quelling habit.
Let her be for now, and in time, when business
drags her from watching

how the sunlight hammers the cliffs to silver,
why not see if one of those beermats floating
like the tips of islands has remnants of her
shining in biro.

# Seferis people-watching in a Cairo bar

Soldiers and street girls, petals like slow fires
burning in palm oil,
answer his tea, its remote swirls touched
with occasions of light. Watch
how, in their leaving, they're journeys about
to be realised, narrative
held in abeyance, apart, for so long
and then boom, with the limelight

burning. Or travellers, smiling across
the aloofness of corner
tables. An argonaut's mind in its own right
nods in the way land
rises from water, and years to be spent wanting
until you lose sight,
losing the processes sight needs. Sometimes
he knows they're more myths

lifted and let go, seabirds, or paper
in sail shapes, each fresh
meat for the khamseen. A waiter, who hobbles
on shrapnel, accepts change
crosses the beermat-defined space, leaning
away to the one true
river. The spark in his thank you reminds
the observer of struck flint,

hubcaps on kerbstones, the images there
and dismissed with the same speed.
Normal conditions return his epiphany's
flash to the flat stone. Fragments attempt
to ignite him again when the best of the girls
who patrol where the war drinks
tries to reflect his directionless staring,
remembers there's no point,

not with a man who completely refuses
to stop with that crap, stop
calling her Cairo's Calypso. Enough yes?
More than enough. God!
Greece is for dead men. Greece stinks. This
is what matters, her hand slapped
hard on the nub of her hip, and the hate
in her throat like a reed flute.

## Cavafy returns to Liverpool

He stops at every statue's fractured sky
and tries to gauge which angle best describes
their impact over time, his camera, shy
at first, avoiding awkwardness. He bribed
an old acquaintance working as a guide
to passing fancy at the Walker: tea,
plus half an hour's discussion, stirring up
their pasts, indulging that undivided
illusion needed now to let it feel
as if they mattered more than shadowed birds

just sliding on the surface, not touching,
or not affecting. Yes, of course he could
just nose around. Why statues though, so much
respect, or was it love, for what just holds on?
He hadn't answered then, preferring time
to think it through among the solid ghosts
of lost ambition, finding answers there
evaporate. He's drawn to those sublime
occasions where a line controls the pose,
suspended moments seeming unaware

of their importance. All those heads of state
attract him too, but more for dated reasons,
those points at which the world was getting late
despite itself. Behind their stares the seas
gush and batter, forcing their changes through
attrition more than anything else. Rome,
Greece, and Victorian ideals agitate
his lens. Outside the building, on show,
one Michelangelo leans beneath a dome
the weather sits on, the gulls like white flags,

the weather blown across the city, smoke
crusting over. Cavafy takes the white
Carrara marble reborn. The parts worn
away will hardly notice once the light's

obliging. Drinking later in the town
he'll play the *flâneur*, he and his old friend,
whose question lit the stone that afternoon.
They'll talk in photographs, his own, and ones
arranged in fleets along the wall, blending
his straw hat with the background laughter

at the bar. Beside them, also laughing,
a man they've not met might accept a rose,
holding the moment by the stem, grafting
to the flower, his pulse, his breathing, slowed.
Or toss it back towards the giver's hand
and watch him go, a bruise the pub window
won't forget. Either way, he'll catch the eye
and know it too, sense it in the two friends,
seated by then, one of them pretending
he hasn't seen, he hasn't realised.

# Salvator Mundi

Never having set eyes on those described as
being almost alive, Vasari also
tells us how he can feel the blood convulsing
in the throat, and the human skin perspiring.
Either someone was sent to see it for him,
or that throb in an attic all those dark years
reached beyond itself to burn the varnishes
back from what's been confirmed as walnut panel.
Did he find he was shocked from sleep, that face glowing
through his own in the mirror? Nothing passive,
nothing patient as stones in that seduction
having sensed in the man a locked potential,
knowing beauty unwitnessed suffocates. Glimpsed
through sfumato exteriors he'd be seen
more for what his assessment might betoken,
any fuss he could make. He'd be manoeuvred
into writing it real, a thing of living
flesh, desires, a dismantled stink of bodies
pulled to fibre on bone, the patterns of trees,
planets, coral, the workings flowers exhibit

torn apart. He'd be writing out of habit,
yet he'd feel how the words unrolled more freely
than his own. As he gripped his quill, he'd model
how the fingers he'd written of hold their gift,
bless the light with their simple gesture moving
his. He'd know how the symbols work once broken
down to meanings: the way the central star gleams
resurrection; the way a ruby's shimmer
shows the depth of the martyr's passion sensing
what's to come; and the way the robe's been tucked in
near the right with a spear in mind. Amassing
what he didn't already know could show us
even more once the oil began its dancing,
tugging hard on the want he'd be harnessed by,
finding him out in what he'd always most feared.
Pointless trying to block the vision thawing

under ad-hoc attempts to paint it out. Fire
shines through marble. A sacred stillness pulses,
not so much with unlikely good, as calling
out the miracle of its own revival.

# Browsing at Jon Wright's bookshop

*Shakespeare finding King Lear*

Before the church, the market stinking up
the street, and magpies squabbling over scraps
of meat and fish. A bookshop calls him out
of beery sleep, the tavern talk of kings
with spending on the brain, the tug of war
distending love so far beyond the gold
they always give it in the poems, poxed
affairs, his same old. Heavy after nights
in Southwark, all the shit of living hard
disintegrates to books and scrolls. In one
he flicks over a heath a world away
exploring limits of the wind. A man
in mud and flowers sings, his voice creaking
its grief. A roughish thing, the play he finds
without a writer, full of what it means
to reach that age when all that's left a man
is hearing what he wants, how much he's loved
to death by sometime daughters. He takes the book
to stow in case, and leaves to face the mixed
clamours and smells of Newgate. Bells extol
their ancient virtues, empty out. Black clouds
collide and squeeze angles of yellow light
between them. Metal squints on buckles, hilts,
the ruffled bronze of puddles. One reaches
towards him with twists of white beard, the slicing
vision born of another way of knowing
what makes a grass-head weigh so much more than
him. A cliff shivers in the stone of the church walls
and their endless falling. Deeper in, pain
rolls its eyes to turmoiling clouds, opens
its soul across a limp girl with her hair
tumbling from her chalk-white, her blue kisses.

# Marian Halcombe

Set against that gentleness Laura carries
out of all proportion to events, Marian
more than compensates, to the point the other
fades to the whiteness

over time deprived of the sun. It's spirit,
ballsy strength of mind, we're in desperate need of
even just a couple of chapters in, hands
able to open

jars of pickles weeks in the larder, shaking
so you'd know it, wearing her introduction
like a bruise for days. There's a hint of Moorish
wildness to mark her

down as having drifted from those domestic
lines expressed so fully in Laura's breeding,
polite reference stressing her *half* of sister,
daughter we never

learn the rest of. A story starting way back
where a servant catches some portrait's gazing
down the wall with more than a passing interest
ends in the managed

shock, the use of *ugly* on nearly bumping
into such an awkwardly put together
female. Once we know, we're as bad in looking
harder and longer

than we should, redeeming ourselves by blurting
something daft she's bound to have lasered straight through
if she's as gross as that, as disturbing, judgment
based on the difference

surely being hardly an unexpected
starting point by now. And especially given
what becomes admission that *ugly* doesn't
always, in this case

anyway, imply she's as vague as Laura,
say, or any other of those insipid
profiles swooning behind an admiration
over their milk-white

shoulders. Try it on with a Marian, swooning's
up to you, or Laura. But making Marian
swear to love her sister above a whole fleet
hers for the taking

smacks of opportunity frittered on trust,
on a weary honesty when there's so much
more she could be seen for, a perfect woman
waiting to happen.

# Elgar's Cello Concerto

Another who felt the changes
deeply, if that tugging is his
when the music in the distance
swells, responding by arrangement

to some overwhelming pressure.
And yet, for all its cataclysm,
turning inwards, where it matters
more than we can ever measure

just by listening. We'd need to be
that old man with the space unfilled
watching a flower which seemed still
tremble. Even then, would we see

in that the drama of letters
loving his precious Windflower
time and again, the hours grinding
against them? Among the petals

stirring with deceptive currents
unnoticed by the tops of trees
there are so many unreleased
images. Setting his flower

by a railway line with a train
waiting near a country station
infers a sense of power placed
against the natural, a straining

with only one result. A brake
relaxes in a hiss of steam.
He could share his seat with someone,
a soldier maybe, for the sake

of it, with a grey smile sliding
from his mouth, missing his moment
and half an arm. As an omen
it serves, like the cello's gliding

towards awareness of its own
wood, its distraught fragility.

## Lowry's loneliest house

To walk towards and not move closer
on a road arching over dun hills,

but maintaining always the constant course
with its nominal end. A house, a white

and remote house, but not pure
you understand, an omniscient china

or lead white, a static monolith
of sulphuric sky to be leant into

by figures chewed out from the inside,
self-absorbed as boned balloons.

But not here. This is not a factory
or a working funeral's last sniff

through the ribs of an iron rail. No one
bends against the grain of this land,

shares its bleached road. Should you reach
his house, it will not know you from the wind.

## Austin's blackbird

*after 'The Blackbird of Derrycairn'*

Austin, did I tell you, your blackbird last night
sang the sun's descending with notes like burst fruit?
Something else. It seemed to me closer, stronger
breaking the late hush,

or was that the night as opposed to time sung
real. You'd know, of course, with the music's echo
ringing louder written than any church bell
swinging its great head.

You, you heard it better. No bough-top needed
here though, just the balance a gutter gave it
killing any chance of escaping. Raw sound
poured through the French door,

minutes filled with nothing except its last song.
Like you said, there's knowledge enough just hearing.
How it carries with it a myth belonging
purely to land, thorn,

time before old Patric came sailing over,
that's the part you lose me. It's only rarely,
autumn's clearer days with a helpful wind, bells
carry the half mile.

Hardly ever. Mostly the blackbird sounds off
sitting high inside the remaining hawthorn.
Last night, though, it chose for its perch the gutter.
Last night it rang true.

## Stephen Hero catches a glimpse of someone

Strolling Eccles Street has become a habit
as we join our hero with art and beauty
making light of what, on another evening,
would have him, not lost,

but in keeping with the indifferent weather.
Drizzle mostly, catches an odd reflection
here and there from one of the recent street-lights,
otherwise, what's left

once the sun and buildings collude, their red glow.
Nothing's certain, family aside, and mulling
over what he shouldn't have said to Emma
seeing her stood there

through Italian lessons and college windows,
rushing stairs, then trying to rush her raincoat,
letting hindsight shine as the clever bastard
once she'd just clammed up.

No chance. Like a girl as completely rigid,
holy polite could be informed the moment
mattered more than God, they should let it happen,
like she just would. Christ's

always got there first, and the smile of someone
knowing what the truth, or as close as makes no
difference, really sounds like. Our route's the usual,
joining the last souls

heading home from work, and the first with money
crossing over, set for the Monto maybe.
Are we, then, supposed to accept that women
have a unique sight,

some intense stupidity men, our hero,
hadn't even touched? With the question rolling
Grafton Street's approaching, the brown of brickwork
Stephen will paint drab

when he gets the chance, an iconic image
meaning life's paralysis, total thought-death,
anyway. A girl from a window hollers
down to her young man.

Light defines her, leaving her words in splinters:
*Wicked* this, and *Chapel on Sundays*, something
giggled brightly over. Our hero's wanting
paper, a good pen,

wanting her to say it again. Her thisness
fills the spaces left by the desperate groping
pushed to walking, minutes, a morning was it?
since on the wet green.

## *Albert Richards, war artist, 1919–1945*

Looking, he says, for that perfect picture
catching the German army in retreat,
the point at which the march turns
a heel-mark in the summer. He's found their horses

in an orchard, their table-legs sticking out
from bloat bellies. A boy there was
in one town tying a tricolor
to an iron rail, and men like reddlemen

part of the machine making din
from iron ore. A landing strip
grew from a concrete cross on fields
screaming with gold fire. Elsewhere

Horsa gliders, piled up,
poking the picture's eye out
with their cardboard tails, their insignia still ours
in a dozen parts. He takes a Jeep

and his colours to the night, the dark
strafed with the ticks of crayoned bullets,
the night which rumbles wire over Caen,
or buckles slabs of itself in the foreground

of another pretty town. He sees
people move like grass, people
shift and vanish in the billows of so much
sky. Hills suit him, let him

peer down through candle-wax explosions
into tiny lives, lives that slide
on green tiles. Or the view through the bay-door
of a plane, of his Jeep in a Dutch field

folding his portrait of himself in flames.

## Dylan Thomas *by Augustus John*

They fought once, rather famously,
over a girl with the glamour
and the tameless abandon
a dancer seems to live by. Brawled
on a carpark, they did, rolling
there like toddlers in the sand

off Fishguard bay. The painter socked
Thomas, sending the golden locks,
seen here looking Alexander's
in a mirror, sprawling. He sat
for him about two years later,
puppy fat reprimanded

by the wet light, and the blubber
of his lips between a baby's,
and the public pretending
it's what you do if you're that way
touched, afflicted. Needless to say
any grazes had mended

by then, so much there's a murmur
of compassion as the brush turns
a pink corner to showy
kisses of precocious breath, sweat
like peaches gone a little bit
off their sweet. John would've known

that bluish prediction, not least
from having picked up the pieces
of a wheezing Innes, blown
from the Fawr up at Arenig
where their painting mattered. That sheen,
that wax skin, it gives its own

account. It shadows like the crows
in a van Gogh, the dirty glow
dinged yellow of Lowry's skies.
It's easy being tender, when,
like the mountain, you've that same sense
of impending destiny.

But for all that, for what it's worth,
Thomas got up to get the girl
and the syrup of eyes full
and open as a mooning cow's.
To look at him with his girl's brow
you'd think snow just wouldn't melt.

# A visit from the ogre

*for R.S. Thomas, 'the ogre of Wales'*

If you ask in one of his quiet moments
he'll tell you how, as the day was closing
his house with dark from the hills, and how,
as he read alone, it was him again,
come alive. The time must've stopped. It does,
or it can. You find, as you glance up, light
that was seconds since like a fire igniting
the glass with winces of gold has slid
to the floor. You find yourself frowning over
a word whose shape is a dancer weaving
the semi-dark from a dream. I've seen
how a bird can sit on a window sill
at the edge of life and appear possessed
with a spark it lacked in the garden's sun
not an hour before. It appears to know
from the forms that crowd in a room, the one
with the gift of breath. You'll be sitting like coal
in its seam, and yet, what the bird detects
is that difference held. If you ask, he'll say
it was all of that with the added bonus
of knowing, really, beyond all doubt,
that the bird that tapped at the glass that evening
was him, the poet with hair like snowstorms
and eyes he'd chisel the mountain's out with.
He knew him well, or as well as anyone
could. They'd share a defensive word
as they passed each other with time alert
at their shoulders, fill their opposing corners
like bottled thoughts, be that distance given
away by stars. And it had his name,
which was stranger still. It was him, old Thomas,
as sure as night on the cooling hills.
He was tapping his beak on the sunset's face.

# Looking at a recent collection of Larkin's letters

One reviewer says he could've done
without the bottom fetish, the detail of a skirt
ordered up in the frosted glass of an office,
or a dream he takes as real, a peep-hole
silk rides like an island inside out,

a picture he might've taken with a wank in mind,
as if he'd rather like a statue of the man instead
to pin his words to, to carve them from,
a fridge to magnetise their patterns for passing by
his hermitage on a whim, going through his life

with a little sterilised jazz piping sweetness
on a plastic cake, left, rather thoughtfully,
to a table he might've sipped at, alone with a score-card
declaring the cricket a fruitless draw from the first
coin, not a whiff of woman anywhere

this side of Hull to unclip an anorak,
to tug a fly to, the usual monotonies suiting
the life of any librarian, save this one
melting into his offending letters, and a lover
always delving in the seal and rabbit fur,

steaming in his glasses, pricking his eggshell features
with jabs of sweat, shaking his fish's belly
full of milt where three of them lie together
close as breath misting the lens, close
enough, the man in his element, and two women

he more than wrote to more often than not,
the one who obliged in his office, her skirt, her wriggle
beneath the nothing of a graveyard in an empty town,
and a second, his secretary, gold letters for her name
and witness to the love, to what just remains.

# Woman who looks like Sophia Loren

*Southport Hospital, 1989*

An arrival heralded the week before
as the faintest ripple of broken sun
on the marine lake, John fetching
those of us outside one by one
and then, over the blade edge
of hospital coffee, nostalgic for an unlikely
verging on impossible girl, if I liked
old films, and Sophia Loren.

I freely said yes, I thought so,
especially *The Fall of the Roman Empire*,
Christopher Plummer, swayed by a mania
that could hear the gods in marble rows
laughing, that actually became a god.
Sophia was there as well, preceded
by the chaise longue of her lower lip
and the voice of *Vogue* newly widowed.

Outside again when the debut happens,
horizon salted past its natural life
and the soft rhythm of the passing cars.
John, with a leather wallet, pulls her
into that round-the-corner-reaching light
beloved of painters of small boats.
German, or so John says, and yes
an exact likeness passport-sized.

If it isn't there, then we're back on the ward
under a more constant speculation.
She still glows, but perhaps while blinking
her ostrich lashes. If not, it could dawn on us
she's not unused to being seen,
gently handled by her quarter inch
of white frame, her fresh-looking colour
laughing more wisely, and for so long.

# Ward round

We're lying in the frieze of a Greek sun.
Some artist must have locked it there
pressing too hard with his thumb
so the light does nothing except
remain. Which is not to say that nothing
stirs beyond the ward door. We hear
before we see the glint of water,
metal in water, a pen, a watch-strap,
the angle of someone wearing glasses.

The last of a river drifts by bed-ends
eddying around the wet rock
here and there of a chart. The river
has such a quiet voice, a murmur's
reflection discussing art with a mirror.
There may be gestures where it pauses,
but these, too, have no substance
past the shapes existing in the sheets,
the pottery faces half asleep.

This one seems well enough, a nurse
tells a doctor. We miss the words,
but we're accustomed to their mouthing unconcern,
the measure of their calm. And we've seen them urgent
in the past, rushing across the gravel.
But not today. A museum moves
this way. There are looks from between us
and the ceiling tiles, ones in their time
who've seen so many of these smashed amphorae.

# An apparition of Kenny Dalglish

*Liverpool FC's Melwood training ground, 2011*

Nearly a lover's look across the shoulder
faithfully rendered from a 70s shot
remembers decades of bedroom walls,
the hunter's chance in its canny eye.

Cheek-bones exaggerate black and white,
skin like a tambourine, like you'd want it, like gods,
like generals, like worse couldn't happen
to an always boy in an always field.

Someone else must've worshipped in that fatter time,
brought sprays on purpose to the fence
with the street sleeping, paint-smell on their breath
making each arc of their colour count.

I'm hoping it was done from memory, from wearing
on the artist's back that number seven,
scoring, re-scoring the same goals
to the same commentator's vocal hard-on.

You can see fence panels through the ghost
like a wooden river. Only the shirt and the shorts
get redded in. Or maybe the image
made itself, like Jesus in a potato.

## *Paula Rego's* Gepetto Washing Pinocchio

Where his fingertips work the wood a lustre
only love is entirely understanding
every nuance of, every hour devoted
to the labour at hand, the cloth starts bleeding
out between his unhurried movements, scarlet
in his palms. It's a tricky area, this part,
where he's got to be careful not to press down
over-hard on the ribs. As tender, almost,
as the delicate grain he felt the flinch of
when he held it, without intending to pinch,

by the throat. It's an art, his gentle contact,
every bit as integral, as essential,
as discovering the grove where cherry-wood grows
undisturbed in perfect light and shade, nurtured
by the winds from the south, the water streaming
freshly off the Italian mountains. Nowhere
else it's quite got the same intense profusion;
even when he's been at it days the polish
never gleams with the warmth it conjures up here
under evening and candle-light. A sap tear

rolls a path from the beads of glass he favoured
for the eyes. It defines a path across cheek,
chin, the moisture the lips have started shining
with the dew of, as varnish covers each groove
knocked and gouged in, the lover's bruises waking
to themselves in the pulse of purple wing-tips
curling out of the knotted cherry. Fragrance
now of more than the forest. Smells of real life
coming from its internal coma, hurting
with the light in a room of tools, inertia

piled as branches and logs he'll use for firewood
later. When he's exhausted, sweat- and work-stained,
slumped against the acceptance of his best chair,
sounds will merge in his mind with trees in strong winds,
sails and beams, their disturbing. Hooves will stutter
over floors as they try to learn their power,
fingers too, an arthritic dance, as surface
grows from sheen into hard and soft. He'll dream hands
reaching up and exploring his. A hurried
breath will gradually steady to a hoarse word.

## Paula Rego's Nativity Christmas card

A movement a field discovers in its yielding
up of an uncoupled breath. A gathering
drawn from the starlighting of the pre-dawn, a form
assembled from the formless. The shimmer of the dream
comes real for her in the dome of her belly
as the moment's heat completes its summoning
the squirm inside. Her term rides her
out to the grasses and the great shout
of a voice's wings. A noiseless ringing
in her mind's ear carries the blindness
of a sun trapped in the trick of its one
light. Arms with the warmth and lightness
of summer's stone unencumber around her
wave's beginnings. Fingers too brave
for the soil she holds in hers foil
her first tremors, the hem of her becoming
less and more. Her mother it was
from her grandmother said the land would be ready
in its own time, brimming that knowing
they both shone. And another she blundered
over in the deep of her dreaming, in the sleeping
sight she'd be broken from with the biting sour
on her lips, and her hip-bones moaning
like cattle lost from the gate-posts to the vast
beyond. No end to their wandering
until the gentleness of a palm and the calmness
of its intention defends her face, an extension
of skin, and not skin. Instinct
finds the point where the pain pierces
at its deepest, at hers. A perfect and nerveless
understanding commands the thundering
inside. She lies in the colliding and falling
of feathers, the breath of mountains and heather,
her head resting on a chest as steady
and soft as rocks and seas, and the ease
of that voice again, of man and the moistness
of woman, unchaining, chanting on the plain

where she lies with her legs gasping, her thighs
in sweat and shivers. Love and motherhood
in the voice, a falling, a buoyancy, her calling
in the night, and the need answered. The dancing
of that sound in the grasses and the pounding of the past
on her fever. She feels the surrounding towns
crumble and rise, the reprisals come
from old wars, and then fold away
into the hollows they came from. She follows the grain
through the phases of dew and dust,
herself as a child smiling from the wilderness
as the labour grabs and lets go,
as the blood and the waters blur. She murmurs
the memory of her first words to the one
who cradles the hope she's cracking open.

## Paula Rego's Dybbuk

Even half a season early
would she sense the weight of a bird
settled like a leaf on her stick roof?

Would anyone until a corner of the bedroom
swells inside its nil colour?

A black umbrella shifts in its wings.
A second look turns its shoulder
out of flight. A dead picture-frame

falls and cracks her lover's face
into a glass kiss. And this is her

instantly filled with the bone taste
of a maribou's bill, its skeleton foot
cupping the roll of her right hip

from the thought of her actually wanting it there
inside. Emptied out that long

when instinct remembers what it was
it speeds the blood. It reaches in
right to the splinter, the hint of white

unfixing from the fleshed end. It fetches
its hunger up to gorge again

on something slipped from the eyes and mouth
fluttered and sobbed to the hurting for.
Wedded to the voiceless world it comes

winging and stiff-suited, pinned
in its last best, boned to the surrendered

breath. It stretches its paper hands,
gapes her name underwater,
shakes in the drowning wings her fingers

dig at. Holding to, pushing
against, the hollow frame, squeezing,

and being squeezed. If they could pull
apart, would the two halves
dive back into the same hold,

neither betraying the sculpted gaze,
all the will of a jug of milk?

But if we could imagine it over, would she
even feel, dare we call it
a dove? ascending from its stick-roof?

## Your picture much appreciated

A slick of light over swimming-pool blue
frames a moment. You're leaning on the side
fingers on the concrete rim providing
that anchor you seem to need, smiling through

comparative dark. I can see you've tried
getting over what cameras do to you.
I can see the day before, its red truth
on your bare shoulders, your smile colliding

with the wish you were the one holding it
instead of the one being held there, still
as your own effigy, both unwilling
and wanting to at the same time. The cold

over here forgets itself. I can feel
the heat of an African day unroll
around you, pressing down on the folded
water, the skin I kiss starting to peel.